TRANSMISSIONS AND DRIVE LINES

NATEF Standards Lab Manual—AT 106

Jack Erjavec/Jim Clarke

Vice President, Technology and Trades SBU:
Alar Elken

Editorial Director:
Sandy Clark

Senior Acquisitions Editor:
David Boelio

Development Editor:
Christopher Shortt

Marketing Director:
Dave Garza

Channel Manager:
Bill Lawrensen

Marketing Coordinator:
Mark Pierro

Production Director:
Mary Ellen Black

Production Manager:
Larry Main

Production Coordinator:
Dawn Jacobson

Project Editor:
Toni Hansen

Art-Design Specialist:
Rachel Baker

Editorial Assistant:
Kevin Rivenburg

COPYRIGHT © 2005 Thomson Delmar Learning. Thomson, the Star Logo, and Delmar Learning are trademarks used herein under license.

Printed in Canada
6 XX 06

For more information contact
Thomson Delmar Learning
Executive Woods
5 Maxwell Drive, PO Box 8007,
Clifton Park, NY 12065-8007
Or find us on the World Wide Web at
www.delmarlearning.com

ALL RIGHTS RESERVED. No part of this work covered by the copyright hereon may be reproduced in any form or by any means—graphic, electronic, or mechanical, including photocopying, recording, taping, Web distribution, or information storage and retrieval systems—without the written permission of the publisher.

For permission to use material from the text or product, contact us by
Tel.   (800) 730-2214
Fax   (800) 730-2215
www.thomsonrights.com

Library of Congress Cataloging-in-Publication Data:
Card Number:

ISBN: 1-4018-8115-7

NOTICE TO THE READER

Publisher does not warrant or guarantee any of the products described herein or perform any independent analysis in connection with any of the product information contained herein. Publisher does not assume, and expressly disclaims, any obligation to obtain and include information other than that provided to it by the manufacturer.

The reader is expressly warned to consider and adopt all safety precautions that might be indicated by the activities herein and to avoid all potential hazards. By following the instructions contained herein, the reader willingly assumes all risks in connection with such instructions.

The publisher makes no representation or warranties of any kind, including but not limited to, the warranties of fitness for particular purpose or merchantability, nor are any such representations implied with respect to the material set forth herein, and the publisher takes no responsibility with respect to such material. The publisher shall not be liable for any special, consequential, or exemplary damages resulting, in whole or part, from the readers' use of, or reliance upon, this material.

CONTENTS

Introduction Information Sheet	1
Table 1 / Clutch Troubleshooting Chart	2

CHAPTER 35 Clutches

Information Sheet / Clutches	5
Job Sheet AT 106-1 / Troubleshoot a Clutch Assembly (Ch. 35)	7
Job Sheet AT 106-2 / Clutch Removal (Ch. 35)	13
Job Sheet AT 106-3 / Clutch Inspection and Servicing (Ch. 35)	17
Job Sheet AT 106-4 / Clutch Reassembly and Installation (Ch. 35)	23
Case Studies	25
Review Questions	27

CHAPTER 36/37 Manual Transmission/Transaxle Service

Information Sheet / Manual Transmission / Transaxle Service	29
Job Sheet AT 106-5 / Identifying Bearings (Ch. 36, 37)	31
Job Sheet AT 106-6 / Power Flow and Component ID (Ch. 36, 37)	35
Job Sheet AT 106-7 / Inspecting Fluid Level (Ch. 36, 37)	37
Job Sheet AT 106-8 / Overhauling a Manual Transmission (Ch. 36, 37)	39
Case Studies	42
Review Questions	43

CHAPTER 38 Drive Axles and Differentials

Information Sheet / Drive Axles and Differentials	45
Job Sheet AT 106-9 / Constant Velocity Joints (Ch. 38)	47
Job Sheet AT 106-10 / Drive Axle Inspection & Diagnosis (Ch. 38)	51
Job Sheet AT 106-11 / Servicing Outer CV joints (Ch. 38)	53
Job Sheet AT 106-12 / Servicing Inner CV joints (Ch. 38)	59
Job Sheet AT 106-13 / Inspecting U-Joints & Driveshafts (Ch. 38)	65
Job Sheet AT 106-14 / Measure & Adjust Pinion Depth, Bearing Preload, and Backlash (Ch. 38)	71
Case Study	73
Review Questions	78

CHAPTER 41 Four and All-Wheel Drive

Information Sheet / Four and All-Wheel Drive	79
Job Sheet AT 106-15 / Inspect Fluid Level in a Transfer Case (Ch. 41)	81
Job Sheet AT 106-16 / Replace a Transfer Case Output Shaft Bushing and Seal (Ch. 41)	83

Job Sheet AT 106-17 / Servicing Locking Hubs (Ch. 41)	87
Case Study	88
Review Questions	89
ASE Prep Test	91

INFORMATION SHEET

TRANSMISSIONS AND DRIVE LINES

The vehicle's clutch, transmission/transaxles, and drive line form the mechanical link between the engine and the driving wheels. These systems contain precision parts such as: gears, joints, and shafts, which are precision meshed and must be carefully serviced and accurately assembled and adjusted. Many of these components can be easily damaged if mishandled or careless.

Transmission/transaxle and drive line components are quite heavy and often difficult to handle and maneuver. Always use the proper safety equipment such as a transmission jack, well-maintained hoist equipment, and recommended disassembly tools.

The manual transmission/transaxle and four-wheel-drive lines contain many components that must be serviced on a regular basis. Components include: clutches, flywheels, bearings, and linkage, universal joints, and transfer cases. The job sheets contained in this section will cover these and related components.

Not all areas of the job sheets in this section may pertain to the particular manual transmission/transaxle, differential, or transfer case that may be assigned to you. It is important to use the correct service information and notes given to you by your instructor to ensure that you are working safely and using the proper procedures in completing your job sheets.

Additional information relating to this subject can be found in the AUTOMOTIVE TECHNOLOGY book, Chapters 35 through 38.

Transmissions and Drive Lines

Table 1 Clutch Troubleshooting Chart

Symptom	Possible Cause	Remedy
Pedal fails to release.	Improper linkage adjustment	Adjust linkage.
	Improper pedal	Trim bumper stop and adjust linkage.
	Loose linkage or worn cable	Replace as necessary.
	Faulty pilot bearing	Replace bearing.
	Faulty clutch disc	Replace clutch disc.
	Fork off ball stud	Install properly and lubricate fingers at release bearings.
	Clutch disc hub binding or input shaft spline	Repair or replace clutch input shaft and/or clutch disc.
	Clutch disc warped or bent	Replace clutch disc.
	Pivot rings loose, broken, or worn	Replace cover and pressure plate assembly.
Slipping.	Improper adjustment	Adjust linkage.
	Oil-soaked clutch disc	Install new disc and correct leak at its source.
	Worn facing or facing torn from clutch disc	Replace clutch disc.
	Warped pressure plate or flywheel	Replace pressure plate or flywheel.
	Weak diaphragm spring	Replace pressure plate.
	Clutch disc not seated	Make 30–40 normal starts. **CAUTION: Do not overheat.**
	Clutch disc overheated	Allow to cool. Check lash.
Grabbing or chattering.	Oil on facing. Burned or glazed facings	Install new clutch disc and correct leak.
	Worn splines on input shaft	Replace input shaft.
	Loose engine mountings	Tighten or replace mountings.
	Warped pressure plate or flywheel	Replace pressure plate and flywheel.
	Burned or smeared resin on flywheel or pressure plate	Sand off if superficial, replace burned or heat-checked parts.
Rattling or transmission click.	Weak retracting springs	Replace pressure plate.
	Clutch fork loose on ball stud or in bearing groove	Inspect ball stud and retainer.
	Oil in clutch plate damper	Replace clutch disc.
	Clutch disc damper spring failure	Replace clutch disc.

Table 1 Continued

Symptom	Possible Cause	Remedy
Release bearing noise with clutch fully engaged.	Improper adjustment	Replace clutch pressure plates.
	Release bearing on transmission bearing retainer	Clean, relubricate, and check for burrs, nicks, etc.
	Insufficient tension between clutch fork spring and ball stud	Replace fork.
	Fork improperly installed	Install properly.
	Weak linkage return spring	Replace spring.
Noisy bearing.	Worn clutch bearing	Replace bearing.
	Springs weak in pressure plate	Replace pressure plate.
	Pilot bearing loose in crankshaft	Refit or replace bearing.
Pedal stays on floor when disengaged.	Bind in cable or clutch bearing	Replace cable.
	Springs weak in pressure plate	Replace pressure plate.
	Springs being overtraveled	Adjust linkage to get proper lash. Be sure proper pedal stop (bumper) is installed.
Pedal hard to depress.	Bind in linkage	Lubricate and free up linkage.
	Clutch disc worn	Replace clutch disc.
	Friction in cable	Replace cable.

INFORMATION SHEET

Clutches

INFORMATION

A clutch has two primary purposes: to mechanically connect the engine's crankshaft to the transmission, and to disconnect the engine's crankshaft from the transmission. The clutch assembly is mounted to the engine's flywheel and is engaged and disengaged by movement of the clutch pedal. This is accomplished by the use of various types of linkage systems. The most common types are cable-type, hydraulic, and lever-type.

Clutch adjustment or service is required whenever the clutch pedal free play is not correct, or when the clutch does not operate properly. Normal clutch wear is adjusted for in the linkage. On most modern vehicles this is accomplished by the use of automatic slack adjusters in the case of cable-type, hydraulically in the case of hydraulic-type, or manual adjustment in the case of lever-type. Clutch adjustment must be done whenever the clutch assembly is removed from the vehicle for repair or replacement.

Troubleshooting the clutch (Table 1) involves checking for clutch chatter, slippage, pulsation, and vibration. Service of the clutch assembly includes a thorough inspection of all components and replacement or refurbishment to restore proper operation. Components needing replacement or refurbishment include: flywheel, throw-out bearing, clutch disc, pressure plate, clutch fork, linkage, and hydraulic parts. The transmission bell housing and rear of the engine block must also be inspected and must align with each other properly.

Clutches 7

☐ JOB SHEET / AT 106-1

Troubleshoot a Clutch Assembly

Name _____ Station _____ Date _____

Objective

Upon completion of this job sheet, you will have demonstrated the ability to troubleshoot a clutch assembly.

Refer to **Chapter 35** in the AUTOMOTIVE TECHNOLOGY book for additional information.

You must be able to perform these task(s) in order to pass the **ASE** test for: **Manual Drive Lines and Axles**

These job sheets meet the requirements for **NATEF** task(s): **Manual Drive Lines and Axles**

Tools and Materials:
AUTOMOTIVE TECHNOLOGY 4e (Thomson, Delmar Learning)
Droplight
Hoist
Pry bar
Ruler
Service manual
Socket set
Wheel chocks
Wrenches

NATEF TASKS
III. Manual Drive Lines and Axles
Category: A
Task: 1 (P-1)
Task: 2 (P-1)
Task: 3 (P-1)
Category B
Task: 1 (P-1)
Task: 2 (P-1)

Protective Gear:
Goggles or safety glasses with side shields

WARNING: *Be sure that the wheels are chocked properly and that the brake system is in good operating condition before beginning this task. Do not allow anyone to stand in front of or behind the vehicle during this test. Do not take any longer than necessary to determine if a problem exists.*

Describe the vehicle being worked on:
Year _____ Make _____ Model _____
VIN _____ Engine type and size _____

PROCEDURE (CHECK CLUTCH CHATTER)

1. Start the engine, set the parking brake, depress the clutch pedal fully, and shift the transmission into first gear. Increase the engine speed to about 1500 rpm, and slowly release the clutch pedal. When the pressure plate first makes contact with the clutch disc, notice the clutch operation. Depress the clutch pedal and reduce the engine speed. Record the results on the Report Sheet for Clutch Troubleshooting, found at end of Job Sheet.   ☐ Task completed

2. Shift the transmission into reverse and repeat step 1. Record the results on the Report Sheet for Clutch Troubleshooting.   ☐ Task completed

3. If clutch chatter does not occur, increase the engine speed to about 2000 rpm and repeat steps 1 and 2. Record the results on the Report Sheet for Clutch Troubleshooting.   ☐ Task completed

4. If chatter occurs during the tests, raise the vehicle on a hoist. Check for loose or broken engine mounts, loose or missing bellhousing bolts, and damaged linkage. Record the results on the Report Sheet for Clutch Troubleshooting. Correct any problems found during the inspection. ☐ Task completed

5. Lower the vehicle and repeat steps 1–3. ☐ Task completed

PROCEDURE (CHECK CLUTCH SLIPPAGE)

1. Block the front wheels with wheel chocks and set the parking brake. Start the engine and run it for 15 minutes or until it reaches normal operating temperature. ☐ Task completed

2. Shift the transmission into high gear and increase the engine speed to about 2000 rpm. Release the clutch pedal slowly until the clutch is fully engaged. ☐ Task completed

   CAUTION: *Do not keep the clutch engaged for more than five seconds at a time. The clutch parts could become overheated and be damaged.*

3. If the engine does not stall, raise the vehicle on a hoist and check the clutch linkage. Correct any problems found during the inspection. Record the results on the Report Sheet for Clutch Troubleshooting. ☐ Task completed

4. If any linkage problems were found and corrected, repeat steps 1 and 2. Record any problems in clutch operation on the Report Sheet for Clutch Troubleshooting. ☐ Task completed

PROCEDURE (CHECK CLUTCH DRAG)

NOTE: *The clutch disc and input shaft require about three to five seconds to come to a complete stop after engagement. This is known as "clutch spindown time." This is normal and should not be mistaken for clutch drag.*

1. Start the engine, depress the clutch pedal fully, and shift the transmission into first gear. ☐ Task completed

2. Shift the transmission into neutral, but do not release the clutch pedal. ☐ Task completed

3. Wait 10 seconds. Shift the transmission into reverse. ☐ Task completed

4. If the shift into reverse causes gear clash, raise the vehicle on a hoist. Record the results on the Report Sheet for Clutch Troubleshooting. ☐ Task completed

5. Inspect the clutch linkage. ☐ Task completed

6. If any linkage problems were found and corrected, repeat steps 1–3. ☐ Task completed

PROCEDURE (CHECK PEDAL PULSATION)

1. Start the engine. Slowly depress the clutch pedal until the clutch just begins to disengage. ☐ Task completed

   NOTE: *A minor pulsation is normal.*

   Depress the clutch pedal further, and check for pulsation as the clutch pedal is depressed to a full stop. Record the results on the Report Sheet for Clutch Troubleshooting.

2. If no rubbing problems are found, remove one drive belt. Start the engine and check for vibration. Shut off the engine. Repeat this process, removing the drive belts and checking for vibration after each drive belt is removed. If the vibration stops after a particular belt is removed, the problem is in the unit driven by that belt. ☐ Task completed

   CAUTION: *Do not run the engine for more than one minute when checking for a vibration with belts removed.*

3. If a vibration is still present, check for a damaged crankshaft vibration damper. Record the results on the Report Sheet for Clutch Troubleshooting. ☐ Task completed

Problems Encountered

_____
_____
_____

Instructor's Comments

_____
_____
_____

Name _____ Station _____ Date _____

REPORT SHEET FOR CLUTCH TROUBLESHOOTING		
1. Pedal freeplay		
Clutch pedal height specification		
Actual pedal height		
Clutch pedal freeplay specification		
Actual pedal freeplay		
2. Clutch chatter test		
	Yes	*No*
First gear 1500 rpm		
Reverse gear 1500 rpm		
First gear 2000 rpm		
Reverse gear 2000 rpm		
3. Visual inspection		
	Serviceable	*Nonserviceable*
Engine mounts		
Transmission mounts		
Transmission crossover		
Bellhousing bolt torque		
Trans. to bell housing bolt torque		
Clutch linkage		
Oil leakage onto disc		

(continued)

12 Clutches

Name _____ Station _____ Date _____

4. Retest for clutch chatter		
	Yes	*No*
First gear 1500 rpm		
Reverse gear 1500 rpm		
First gear 2000 rpm		
Reverse gear 2000 rpm		
5. Clutch slippage test		
Engine stall		
6. Visual inspection		
	Serviceable	*Nonserviceable*
Linkage adjustment		
Linkage components		
Oil leakage		
7. Clutch drag test		
	Yes	*No*
Gear clash		
8. Pedal pulsation test		
	Yes	*No*
Top of pedal travel		
Freeplay removed		
Middle of travel		
End of travel		

Conclusions and Recommendations _____

_____

_____

REVIEW QUESTIONS

1. List three types of clutch linkages used in modern vehicles.

   a. _____

   b. _____

   c. _____

2. Is minor pulsation a normal condition in typical clutch operation?

   _____

3. Technician A says a stretched clutch cable could cause gear clash during shifting. Technician B says a leaking clutch slave cylinder could cause premature release bearing wear. Who is correct?

   a. Technician A   c. Both A and B
   b. Technician B   d. Neither A nor B

4. Why must the pressure plate retaining bolts be loosened a little at a time in a rotating pattern?

   _____

   _____

5. List four possible causes of clutch slippage.

   a. _____

   b. _____

   c. _____

   d. _____

6. When installing a new release bearing, Technician A says the outer surface of the transmission's front bearing retainer should be lubricated. Technician B says the release lever and pivot should be lubricated. Who is correct?

   a. Technician A   c. Both A and B
   b. Technician B   d. Neither A nor B

7. What safety precautions must be taken concerning dust in the bellhousing?

   _____

   _____

8. Describe the procedure for checking clutch pedal free travel.

   _____

   _____

9. While discussing the possible causes for damage to the surface of a pressure plate, Technician A says a worn clutch disc can score the surface. Technician B says insufficient pedal free travel can cause it to overheat. Who is correct?

   a. Technician A   c. Both A and B
   b. Technician B   d. Neither A nor B

10. List three possible causes of a noisy bearing during clutch operation.

   a. _____

   b. _____

   c. _____

INFORMATION SHEET

Manual Transmission/Transaxle Service

INFORMATION

Today's manual transmissions/transaxles are constant-mesh, fully synchronized designs. Most of them are five speed gearboxes, although a few have four or six speeds. In basic operation, a transaxle functions in the same way as a transmission. The difference between the two is that the transaxle contains the final drive assembly.

A transmission is a collection of gears and shafts. The gears allow for changes in drive speeds and torque. The gears are either part of the shaft assembly or ride on the shafts. When gears ride on the shaft, bearings are used to minimize friction. Bearings, of course, are also used to support the shafts while allowing them to rotate.

When a gear ratio is selected, the speed gear is locked to the output shaft and power is transmitted from the input shaft to that gear and the output shaft. A shift fork accomplishes the locking of a speed gear to the shaft. The shift linkage moves the shift forks, which can be either internal or external.

The shift fork moves a collar of a synchronizer assembly so that a connection is made between the synchronizer and the speed gear. The speed gear normally freewheels on the shaft. The drive gear of the synchronizer is firmly secured to the shaft. When the collar moves to connect the synchronizer to the gear, the speed gear moves with the synchronizer and the shaft.

The primary purpose of the synchronizer is to prevent the gears from clashing and damage while the driver is shifting gears. It does this by synchronizing the speed of the selected gear with the speed of the shaft.

Manual Transmission/Transaxle Service **31**

☐ JOB SHEET / AT 106-5

Identifying Bearings

Name _____   Station _____   Date _____

Objective

Upon completion of this job sheet, you will demonstrate the ability to correctly identify the bearings found in a typical manual transmission/transaxle.

Refer to **Chapter 35 through 38** in the AUTOMOTIVE TECHNOLOGY book for additional information.

You must be able to perform these task(s) in order to pass the **ASE** test for: **Manual Drive Lines and Axles**

These job sheets meet the requirements for **NATEF** task(s): **Manual Drive Line and Axles**

Tools and Materials:
AUTOMOTIVE TECHNOLOGY 4e (Thomson, Delmar Learning)
All-Data®
Service manual
Instructor notes

NATEF TASKS
III. Manual Drive Lines and Axles
Category: C
Task: 4 (P-2)

Protective Gear:
Safety glasses or goggles as required

Describe the vehicle being worked on:
Year _____ Make _____ Model _____
VIN _____ Engine type and size _____

PROCEDURE

On a vehicle assigned to you by your instructor, use the service information sources available to identify all of the bearings in the vehicle's transmission or transaxle. List the location of each. For each bearing, determine the speed gear that would operate noisily if the bearing were bad.

1. Bearing location and identification:

   _____

   _____

   a. Speed gear affected by bad bearing

   _____

2. Bearing location and identification:

   _____

   _____

   a. Speed gear affected by bad bearing

   _____

Manual Transmission/Transaxle Service

3. Bearing location and identification:
   _____
   _____

   a. Speed gear affected by bad bearing
   _____

4. Bearing location and identification:
   _____
   _____

   a. Speed gear affected by bad bearing
   _____

5. Bearing location and identification:
   _____
   _____

   a. Speed gear affected by bad bearing
   _____

6. Bearing location and identification:
   _____
   _____

   a. Speed gear affected by bad bearing
   _____

7. Bearing location and identification:
   _____
   _____

   a. Speed gear affected by bad bearing
   _____

Problems Encountered
_____
_____
_____

Instructor's Comments
_____
_____
_____

Manual Transmission/Transaxle Service   33

☐ **JOB SHEET / AT 106-6**

Power Flow and Component Identification

Name _____ Station _____ Date _____

Objective

Upon completion of this job sheet, you will demonstrate the ability to correctly trace the power flow of a typical manual transmission or transaxle, and identify the various parts involved.

Refer to **Chapters 35 through 38** in the AUTOMOTIVE TECHNOLOGY book for additional information.

You must be able to perform these tasks in order to pass the **ASE** test for: **Manual Drive Lines and Axles**

These job sheets meet the requirements for **NATEF** task(s): **Manual Drive Line and Axles**

Tools and Materials:
AUTOMOTIVE TECHNOLOGY 4e (Thomson, Delmar Learning)
All-Data®
Instructor notes or handouts

NATEF TASKS
III. Manual Drive Lines and Axles
Category: A
Task: 2 (P-1)

Protective Gear:
Safety glasses or goggles as required

Describe the vehicle being worked on:
Year _____ Make _____ Model _____
VIN _____ Engine type and size _____

PROCEDURE

On an instructor-designated transmission or transaxle, draw a basic picture of the components, and label them correctly. Also trace a line through the components you have drawn to indicate the flow of power through the transmission/transaxle. Use the space below for your drawing.

Problems Encountered

_____
_____
_____

Instructor's Comments

_____
_____
_____

Manual Transmission/Transaxle Service **35**

☐ JOB SHEET / AT 106-7

Inspect the Fluid Level in a Manual Transmission and Transaxle

Name _____ Station _____ Date _____

Objective

Upon completion of this job sheet, you will have demonstrated the ability to check the fluid level in a manual transmission and transaxle.

Refer to **Chapters 30, 34 and 35** in the AUTOMOTIVE TECHNOLOGY book for additional information.

You must be able to perform these tasks in order to pass the **ASE** test for: **Manual Drive Lines and Axles**

These job sheets meet the requirements for **NATEF** task(s): **Manual Drive Line and Axles**

Tools and Materials:
AUTOMOTIVE TECHNOLOGY 4e (Thomson, Delmar Learning)
Hand tools
Service manual

NATEF TASKS
III. Manual Drive Lines and Axles
Category: A
Task: 4 (P-1)

Protective Gear:
Goggles or safety glasses with side shields

Describe the vehicle being worked on:
Year _____ Make _____ Model _____
VIN _____ Engine type and size _____

PROCEDURE

1. Refer to the service manual to determine the fluid level check point on the specific vehicle you are checking. ☐ Task completed

2. Refer to the service manual to determine the type of fluid for the specific vehicle you are checking. ☐ Task completed

3. The transmission/transaxle gear oil level should be checked at the intervals specified in the service manual. Normally, these range from every 7,500 to 30,000 miles (12070–48280 k). For service convenience, many units are now designed with a dipstick and filler tube accessible from beneath the hood. Check the oil with the engine off and the vehicle resting on level grade. If the engine has been running, wait 2 to 3 minutes before checking the gear oil level. ☐ Task completed

4. Some vehicles have no dipstick. Instead, the vehicle must be placed on a lift and the oil level checked through the fill plug opening on the side of the unit. Clean the area around the plug before loosening and removing it. Insert a finger or bent rod into the hole to check the level. The oil may be hot. ☐ Task completed

Lubricant should be level with, or not more than 1/2 inch (13 mm) below the fill hole. Add the proper grade lubricant as needed using a filler pump.

5. Manual transmission/transaxle lubricants in use today include single and multiple viscosity gear oils, engine oils, synchromesh fluid and automatic transmission fluid. Always refer to the service manual to determine the correct lubricant and viscosity range for the vehicle and operation conditions.   ☐ Task completed

Problems Encountered

___
___

Instructor's Comments

___
___

INFORMATION SHEET

Drive Axles and Differentials

INFORMATION

The output of a transmission or transaxle is transferred to the vehicle's driving wheels through several major components. In a rear-wheel-drive vehicle, these include the drive shaft and rear axle assembly, which consists of the differential and rear drive axles. Front-wheel-drive vehicles use a differential contained in the transaxle, along with the half-shaft drive axles using inner and outer constant velocity joints. Four-wheel-drive vehicles use elements of both front- and rear-wheel drive systems, plus special transfer case gearing to split the driving power between the front- and rear-drive axles.

To transfer power effectively, drive shafts must be balanced and installed at proper operating angles. Drive shaft universal joints and drive axle constant velocity (CV) joints must be properly installed, lubricated, and protected against dirt penetration. Finally, differential gearing must be maintained in good working order, with particular attention given to proper lubrication.

Drive Axles and Differentials 63

☐ JOB SHEET / AT 106-13

Inspecting U-Joints and the Driveshaft

Name _____ Station _____ Date _____

Objective

Upon completion of this job sheet, you will have demonstrated the ability to inspect the components of a RWD driveline, check U-joint angles and driveshaft runout, and balance a driveshaft.

Refer to **Chapter 38** in the AUTOMOTIVE TECHNOLOGY book for additional information.

You must be able to perform these tasks in order to pass the **ASE** test for: **Manual Drive Lines and Axles**

These job sheets meet the requirements for **NATEF** task(s): **Manual Drive Line and Axles**

Tools and Materials:
AUTOMOTIVE TECHNOLOGY 4e (Thomson, Delmar Learning)
Brass drift
Miscellaneous hand tools
Shop towel(s)
Chalk, crayon, or paint stick
Hose clamps
Dial indicator
Torque wrench
Transmission jack
Inclinometer
Service manual

NATEF TASKS
III. Manual Drive Lines and Axles
Category: D
Task: 2 (P-1)
Task: 5 (P-3)
Task: 6 (P-2)

Protective Gear:
Goggles or safety glasses with side shields

Describe the vehicle being worked on:
Year _____ Make _____ Model _____
VIN _____ Engine type and size _____
Describe general condition: _____
_____

PROCEDURE (VISUAL INSPECTION)

1. Place the transmission in neutral and raise the vehicle on a drive-on hoist. Inspect for leaks at the slip joint, U-joints, final drive pinion seal, and pinion companion flange. Record the results on the Report Sheet for Driveline Inspection, found at end of Job Sheet.   ☐ Task completed

64 Drive Axles and Differentials

2. Shake and twist the driveshaft to locate worn or loose parts. Pry with a screwdriver around the U-joints. Record the results on the Report Sheet for Driveline Inspection. ☐ Task completed

3. Check for dirt, undercoating, dents, or missing balancing weights on the driveshaft. Inspect the center-bearing rubber bushing and support bracket, if equipped. Record the results on the Report Sheet for Driveline Inspection. ☐ Task completed

   CAUTION: *Before attempting to check a center bearing, be sure the driving wheels and driveshaft are free to rotate.*

4. Check the center bearing, if equipped. ☐ Task completed

   WARNING: *Extreme care should be taken when working around a rotating driveshaft. Severe injury can result from touching a moving shaft.*

PROCEDURE (CHECK U-JOINT ANGLES)

1. Locate the specification for U-joint angles in the service manual. Clean the surfaces where the inclinometer will be mounted. ☐ Task completed

   CAUTION: *Do not force the inclinometer when setting it into position, or a false reading will be recorded* (Figure 15).

Figure 15. Inspecting driveshaft angles with an inclinometer. *Courtesy of Daimler Chrysler Corporation*

2. Check the front U-joint angle, and record the reading on the Report Sheet for Driveline Inspection. ☐ Task completed

3. Check the rear U-joint angle, and record the reading on the Report Sheet for Driveline Inspection. ☐ Task completed

4. If necessary, correct the U-joint angles. ☐ Task completed

   CAUTION: *Do not use too many shims. Measure at the center of each shim. It should be no thicker than 1/4 inch (6.35 mm). If the rear U-joint angle is not correct, other problems may exist in the suspension. These problems include broken springs or an improperly placed spring seat.*

PROCEDURE (CHECK DRIVESHAFT RUNOUT)

1. Locate the specification for driveshaft runout in the service manual. Clean the areas on the driveshaft where the dial indicator plunger will ride. ☐ Task completed

2. Mount the dial indicator. Take runout readings at each end and at the center of the driveshaft (Figure 16). ☐ Task completed

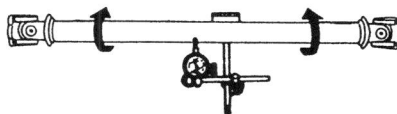

Figure 16. Taking runout readings on a driveshaft.

3. If necessary, disconnect the driveshaft, rotate it 180 degrees on the differential companion flange, and reinstall it. Recheck the runout readings. ☐ Task completed

4. If necessary, replace the driveshaft. Recheck the runout readings. ☐ Task completed

Problems Encountered

_____
_____
_____

Instructor's Comments

_____
_____
_____

Name _____ Station _____ Date _____

	Serviceable	Nonserviceable
REPORT SHEET FOR DRIVELINE INSPECTION		
1. Inspection		
Leaks		
U-joints		
Yokes/Companion flange		
Driveshaft		
2. U-joint angles		
Front angle specification		
Actual front angle		
Rear angle specification		
Actual rear angle		
3. Driveshaft runout		
Maximum runout specification		
Actual runout at front		
Actual runout at middle		
Actual runout at rear		
	Yes	*No*
Conclusions and Recommendations _____		
_____		
_____		

Drive Axles and Differentials 69

☐ **JOB SHEET / AT 106-14**

Measure and Adjust Pinion Depth, Bearing Preload, and Backlash

Name _____ Station _____ Date _____

Objective

Upon completion of this job sheet, you will have demonstrated the ability to inspect, and adjust drive pinion depth, bearing preload, and ring and pinion gear backlash.

Refer to **Chapter 38** in the AUTOMOTIVE TECHNOLOGY book for additional information.

You must be able to perform these tasks in order to pass the **ASE** test for: **Manual Drive Lines and Axles**

These job sheets meet the requirements for **NATEF** task(s): **Manual Drive Line and Axles**

Tools and Materials:
AUTOMOTIVE TECHNOLOGY 4e (Thomson, Delmar Learning)
Hand tools
Dial indicator
Pinion depth gauge
Torque wrench
Service manual
Pinion gear flange holding tool
Micrometer

NATEF TASKS
III. Manual Drive Lines and Axles
Category: E
Task: 1.1 (P-2)
Task: 1.2 (P-2)
Task: 1.3 (P-2)
Task: 1.4 (P-2)
Task: 1.5 (P-2)
Task: 1.6 (P-2)
Task: 1.7 (P-1)
Task: 1.8 (P-1)
Task: 1.9 (P-1)
Task: 1.10 (P-2)
Task: 1.11 (P-2)

Protective Gear:
Goggles or safety glasses with side shields

Describe the vehicle being worked on:
Year _____ Make _____ Model _____
VIN _____ Engine type and size _____

PROCEDURE (DRIVE PINION DEPTH)

1. Inspect the condition of the pinion bearings; replace them if necessary. ☐ Task completed

2. Inspect the pinion gear for any markings indicating additional adjustments. Record the markings: _____

3. Set up the pinion depth gauge according to the procedure outlined in the service manual. ☐ Task completed

4. Set up the dial indicator on the carrier housing. ☐ Task completed

5. Make the necessary readings with the indicator and record the results: ☐ Task completed

6. How much needs to be added or subtracted to achieve proper pinion depth? _____

7. Refer to the service manual to determine the correct size of pinion shim that should be used. ☐ Task completed

8. Install the shim and bearing on the pinion gear shaft. ☐ Task completed

9. Install the pinion gear into the carrier housing. ☐ Task completed

PROCEDURE (PINION BEARING PRELOAD)

1. Install the pinion gear, crush sleeve, and bearing into the carrier housing. ☐ Task completed

2. Install the pinion seal into the housing. ☐ Task completed

3. Install the pinion flange, washer, and nut on the pinion. ☐ Task completed

4. Using the flange holding tool, tighten the pinion nut. ☐ Task completed

5. Using a torque wrench, measure the torque required to turn the pinion gear. Required torque is: _____ ☐ Task completed

6. Refer to the service manual for the proper torque required to turn the pinion. Specified torque is: _____ ☐ Task completed

7. Tighten the pinion nut until the proper torque reading is reached. ☐ Task completed

PROCEDURE (RING AND PINION GEAR BACKLASH)

1. Check the ring gear for runout by setting the dial indicator on the back side of the ring gear. ☐ Task completed

2. Rotate the ring gear one complete revolution and note the movement on the dial indicator. Describe what you observed:
_____
_____

3. What was the highest reading? _____

4. What was the lowest reading? _____

5. Subtract the lowest from the highest; this indicates the total runout of the ring gear. What was it? _____

6. If the runout was not within specifications, check the runout of the carrier before replacing the ring gear. ☐ Task completed

7. Now, install the differential case and ring gear into the carrier housing. ☐ Task completed

8. Mount the dial indicator onto the carrier housing. ☐ Task completed

9. Set the dial indicator on a ring gear tooth. ☐ Task completed

10. Look up the specifications for backlash and record them here:
_____

11. Rock the ring gear back and forth against the teeth of the pinion gear. ☐ Task completed

12. Observe the total movement of the indicator; this is the total backlash. Your readings were: _____

13. Measure backlash at four different spots on the ring gear. ☐ Task completed

14. Describe what needs to happen to correct the backlash:
_____
_____
_____

15. Using knock-in shims or adjusting nuts (depending on axle design), move the ring gear in reference to the pinion gear to achieve proper backlash. ☐ Task completed

16. When proper backlash is reached, torque the retaining caps to specifications. ☐ Task completed

17. Verify the backlash to make sure it is still within specifications. ☐ Task completed

Problems Encountered
_____
_____
_____

Instructor's Comments
_____
_____
_____

CASE STUDY

A customer complains that her rear-drive unit makes noise above 30 mph (50 km) while under load. When coasting, there is no noise. Using the service manual, determine what could be the cause.
_____
_____
_____
_____

REVIEW QUESTIONS

1. What should be done if a damaged CV joint boot is found on a vehicle?

2. Should inboard tripod plunge CV joints be cleaned with solvent or wiped clean with rags? Explain your answer.

3. What is an inclinometer used for?

4. What can result from a dent in a driveshaft?

5. What type of final drive unit gear set requires timing?

6. What is the only acceptable method of removing rear axle shaft bearings and collars?

7. On "C"-lock-type rear axle shafts, where is the lockscrew or bolt located?

8. How is rear axle shaft endplay adjusted?

9. Technician A says drivetrain noise could be caused by pinion bearings. Technician B says it is often difficult to accurately pinpoint drivetrain problems with only a road test. Who is correct?
    a. Technician A
    b. Technician B
    c. Both A and B
    d. Neither A nor B

10. A clunking noise occurs each time the speed gears are changed. Technician A says loose rear control arms could be the cause. Technician B says a worn U-joint could be the cause. Who is correct?
    a. Technician A
    b. Technician B
    c. Both A and B
    d. Neither A nor B

INFORMATION SHEET

Four and All Wheel Drive

INFORMATION

To accomplish four wheel or all wheel drive, additional gearing is needed over and above the transmission/transaxle gearing. This gearing is usually contained in a transfer case. Heavy-duty systems based on rear-wheel-drive setups usually use a separate transfer case remote from the transmission. Vehicles not intended for heavy-duty off-road use usually locate this additional gearing in a smaller transfer case mounted on the back or bottom of the transaxle case.

Gearing principles are similar to those found in manual transmissions. Many systems also use an interaxle or third differential to help equalize power transmission to both the front and rear drivelines during all types of operating conditions

Work safely! Many transaxle cases are extremely heavy, and they contain transmission fluid that can become very hot. All drivelines must be properly supported when disconnected. Rebuilding transfer cases is similar to transmission/transaxle work and is often undertaken as a specialized field. Service performed by the general service technician may include inspection, unit removal and replacement, servicing oil seals and bushings, and replacement of worn hub locking mechanisms.

Four and All Wheel Drive   75

☐ JOB SHEET / AT 106-15

Inspect Fluid Level in a Transfer Case

Name _____ Station _____ Date _____

Objective

Upon completion of this job sheet, you will have demonstrated the ability to properly inspect the fluid in a transfer case.

Refer to **Chapter 41** in the AUTOMOTIVE TECHNOLOGY book for additional information.

You must be able to perform these tasks in order to pass the **ASE** test for: **Manual Drive Lines and Axles**

These job sheets meet the requirements for **NATEF** task(s): **Manual Drive Line and Axles**

Tools and Materials:
AUTOMOTIVE TECHNOLOGY 4e (Thomson, Delmar Learning)
Hand tools
Service manual

NATEF TASKS
III. Manual Drive Lines and Axles
Category: A
Task: 4 (P-1)
Category: F
Task: 6 (P-3)

Protective Gear:
Goggles or safety glasses with side shields

Describe the vehicle being worked on:
Year _____ Make _____ Model _____
VIN _____ Engine type and size _____

Describe the type of system and the model of the transfer case:
_____

PROCEDURE

1. Raise and support the vehicle. ☐ Task completed

2. Locate the fill plug on the transfer case. (Refer to the service manual for the location of the plug.) ☐ Task completed

3. Remove the filler plug. ☐ Task completed

4. Using your little finger, feel in the hole to determine if you can touch the fluid. ☐ Task completed

5. If you cannot touch the fluid, refer to the service manual for fluid type. Fill the transfer case. The recommended fluid is_____ . ☐ Task completed

6. If the transfer case is low on fluid, visually inspect it to locate the leaks. ☐ Task completed

7. If you can reach the fluid with your finger, note the smell, color, and texture of the fluid. ☐ Task completed

8. If the fluid is contaminated, determine what is contaminating it. Then correct that problem and drain the fluid from the transfer case and refill it with clean fluid. ☐ Task completed

Problems Encountered
_____
_____
_____

Instructor's Comments
_____
_____
_____

☐ JOB SHEET / AT 106-16

Replace a Transfer Case Output Shaft Bushing and Seal

Name _____ Station _____ Date _____

Objective

Upon completion of this job sheet, you will have safely and properly demonstrated the ability to replace the bearing oil seal on the rear driveline shaft of a typical four-wheel-drive transfer case (Figure 17).

Refer to **Chapter 41** in the AUTOMOTIVE TECHNOLOGY book for additional information.

You must be able to perform these tasks in order to pass the **ASE** test for: **Manual Drive Lines and Axles**

These job sheets meet the requirements for **NATEF** task(s): **Manual Drive Line and Axles**

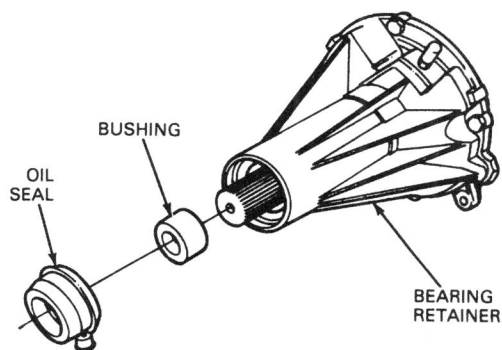

Figure 17. Rear output shaft bearing retainer oil seal and housing. *Courtesy of Ford Motor Company*

Tools and Materials:

AUTOMOTIVE TECHNOLOGY 4e (Thomson, Delmar Learning)
Chalk or marker
Droplight
Extension housing bushing installation tool
Extension housing bushing removal tool
Hammer
Hoist
Multipurpose lubricant or transmission fluid
Screwdriver
Seal installation tool
Service manual
Slide hammer and oil seal removal tool
Socket wrenches and handle
Torque wrench
Wire

NATEF TASKS
III. Manual Drive Lines and Axles
Category: F
Task: 1 (P-3)

Protective Gear:

Goggles or safety glasses with side shields

Describe the vehicle being worked on:

Year _____ Make _____ Model _____
VIN _____ Engine type and size _____

Describe the type of transfer case:
_____

PROCEDURE (REMOVAL OIL SEAL AND BEARING)

1. Raise the vehicle on hoist. ☐ Task completed

   WARNING: *Lifting a four-wheel-drive truck on some hoists requires the use of adapters. Ensure proper pad contact by shaking the vehicle when it is a few inches off the floor. If the vehicle appears to be unstable, lower it and reset the pads.*

2. Using chalk or a marker, index the driveline shaft at the rear axle flange and remove the driveshaft. If required, remove the flange from the transfer case. ☐ Task completed

3. Remove the oil seal from the bearing retainer by prying it with a screwdriver or using a slide hammer and seal removal tool (Figure 18). ☐ Task completed

4. Remove the bushing from the retainer using an extension housing bushing removal tool (Figure 19). Discard both the bushing and the old oil seal. ☐ Task completed

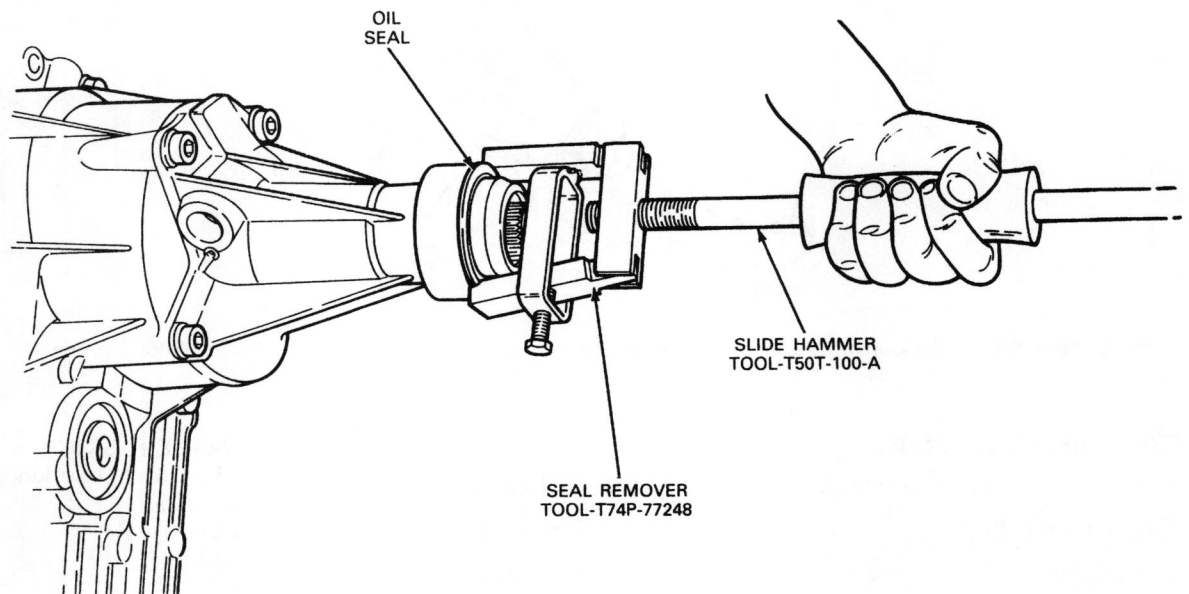

Figure 18. Removing the oil seal from the bearing retainer using a seal removal tool. *Courtesy of Ford Motor Company*

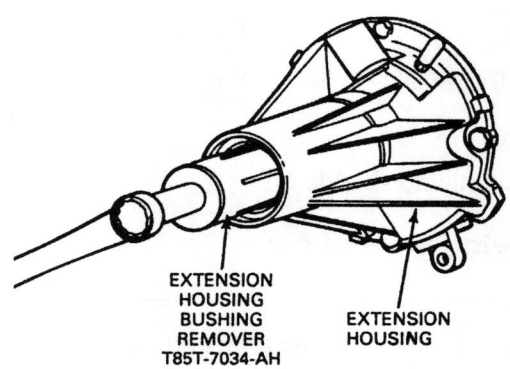

Figure 19. Removing the bushing from the retainer using an extension housing bushing removal tool. *Courtesy of Ford Motor Company*

PROCEDURE (INSTALL NEW BUSHING AND OIL SEAL)

1. Drive the bushing into place in the retainer using an extension housing bushing installation tool (Figure 20). ☐ Task completed

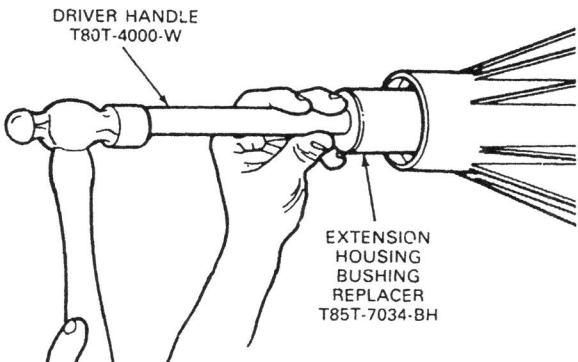

Figure 20. Driving the bushing into place in the retainer using an extension housing bushing installation tool. *Courtesy of Ford Motor Company*

2. Position the seal in the retainer so the notch on the seal faces upward and the drain hole in the rubber dust boot faces downward. Drive the seal in the retainer using a seal installation tool (Figure 21). Replace the flange and torque the nut to specifications. ☐ Task completed

   Torque specification _____

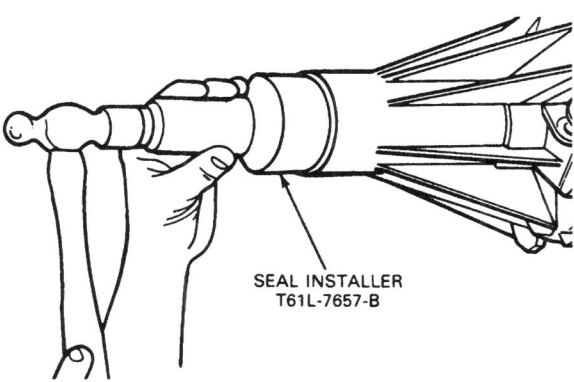

Figure 21. Driving a seal in the retainer using a seal installation tool. *Courtesy of Ford Motor Company*

3. Position the driveline shaft so it aligns with the index marks on the transfer case and rear axles. Install the driveline shaft in the slip splines in the transfer case retainer. Install the driveshaft to the rear axle flange. Tighten the fasteners to the torque specified in the service manual. ☐ Task completed

   Torque specification _____

Problems Encountered

_____
_____
_____

Instructor's Comments

_____
_____
_____

☐ JOB SHEET / AT 106-17

Servicing Locking Hubs

Name _____ Station _____ Date _____

Objective

Upon completion of this job sheet, you will service a four-wheel-drive locking hub assembly.

Refer to **Chapter 35 through 38** in the AUTOMOTIVE TECHNOLOGY book for additional information.

You must be able to perform these tasks in order to pass the **ASE** test for: **Manual Drive Lines and Axles**

These job sheets meet the requirements for **NATEF** task(s): **Manual Drive Line and Axles**

Tools and Materials:
AUTOMOTIVE TECHNOLOGY 4e (Thomson, Delmar Learning)
All-Data®
Instructor notes

NATEF TASKS
III. Manual Drive Lines and Axles
Category: F
Task: 5 (P-3)

Protective Gear:
Safety glasses or goggles as required

Describe the vehicle being worked on:
Year _____ Make _____ Model _____
VIN _____ Engine type and size _____

PROCEDURE

Using the service manual procedures on an instructor assigned vehicle, you will disassemble, clean, inspect, and reassemble a front-wheel-drive locking hub assembly. Record the procedures used and the condition of the parts.

Procedure followed:

_____
_____
_____
_____
_____
_____
_____

Condition of parts:

_____
_____
_____
_____

Problems Encountered

_____
_____
_____

Instructor's Comments

_____
_____
_____

CASE STUDY

A customer complains that no torque is being delivered to the front axle when he shifts his New Process 208 transfer case into four-high or four-low positions. What can be the cause of the problem?

_____
_____

REVIEW QUESTIONS

1. Which type of system, four-wheel drive or all-wheel drive, allows the driver to shift between two-wheel-drive and four-wheel-drive operating modes?
   _____

2. True or false? To provide independent front suspension, some 4WD vehicles have one half shaft and one solid axle for the front drive axle. _____

3. True or false? Some manufacturers use a system whereby selecting 4WD on the selector switch energizes a heating element in the axle disconnect. The heating element heats a gas, causing the plunger to operate the shift mechanism. _____

4. True or false? When the transfer case is shifted into the HIGH position, an additional overdrive gear is added to the driveline. _____

5. Most heavy-duty pick-up trucks and utility vehicles are adapted from what type of base vehicle drivetrain?
   _____
   _____
   _____

6. What is the advantage of using limited slip differentials on the front and rear axle assemblies of four-wheel-drive and all-wheel-drive vehicles not equipped with interaxle differentials?
   _____
   _____
   _____

7. Which of the following statements is not true?
   a. Many newer RWD-based vehicles have an automatic four-wheel-drive feature that switches from 2WD to 4WD when the transfer case shift control module receives wheel rotating slip information from the wheel sensors.
   b. On some vehicles, the driver can select two-, three-, or four-wheel drive by turning the locking hubs at the front wheels.
   c. Some pick-ups and SUVs are fitted with AWD systems that use a viscous clutch as a torque distribution device.
   d. Some truck all-wheel-drive systems rely on a gerotor pump to react to variations between front and rear axle speeds.

8. What is the purpose of a viscous clutch in some transfer case designs?
   _____
   _____

9. While diagnosing the cause of a clunking noise that occurs each time the speed gears are changed, Technician A says loose rear control arms could be the cause. Technician B says a worn U-joint could be the cause. Who is correct?

    a. Technician A
    b. Technician B
    c. Both A and B
    d. Neither A nor B

10. While diagnosing the cause of noise from the transfer case, Technician A says a likely cause is incorrect tire size on one of the drive axles. Technician B says a probably cause is a faulty bearing or gear. Who is correct?

    a. Technician A
    b. Technician B
    c. Both A and B
    d. Neither A nor B

ASE PREP TEST

1. Technician A says the axle hub nut on a FWD vehicle sets the amount of bearing play at the wheel. Technician B says 4WD bearings are normally removed from the steering knuckle after the knuckle has been removed from the car. Who is correct?

   a. Technician A
   b. Technician B
   c. Both A and B
   d. Neither A nor B

2. While discussing the possible causes for a clunking noise heard during acceleration, Technician A says a CV joint could be the cause. Technician B says insufficient ring and pinion gear backlash could be the cause. Who is correct?

   a. Technician A
   b. Technician B
   c. Both A and B
   d. Neither A nor B

3. While reviewing the procedure for replacing an axle boot, Technician A says the position of the old boot should be marked on the shaft prior to removing it. Technician B says that if the boot is dimpled or collapsed after installing it, a dulled screwdriver should be used to allow air to enter the boot. Who is correct?

   a. Technician A
   b. Technician B
   c. Both A and B
   d. Neither A nor B

4. A vehicle makes a loud clunking sound during a left turn; during a right turn, the noise is still apparent but is less pronounced. Technician A says that the left inner CV joint may be the source of the noise. Technician B says the right outer CV joint may be causing the problem. Who is correct?

   a. Technician A
   b. Technician B
   c. Both A and B
   d. Neither A nor B

5. When reviewing the procedure for installing a clutch disc, Technician A says the clutch disc should always be installed with its hub and springs toward the engine. Technician B says the splines of the disc should be clean and never greased or oiled. Who is correct?

   a. Technician A
   b. Technician B
   c. Both A and B
   d. Neither A nor B

6. A bearing-type noise is heard immediately when the clutch pedal is depressed; as the pedal is pushed to the floor the noise remains about the same. When the clutch pedal is released, the noise disappears. Technician A says the clutch pilot bearing could be at fault. Technician B says the clutch release bearing could be at fault. Who is correct?

   a. Technician A
   b. Technician B
   c. Both A and B
   d. Neither A nor B

7. During transmission disassembly and inspection, Technician A checks the condition of the cluster gear thrust washer using a feeler gauge inserted between the end of the cluster gear and the inside wall of the transmission housing. Technician B makes the same check using a dial gauge. Who is correct?

   a. Technician A
   b. Technician B
   c. Both A and B
   d. Neither A nor B

8. A customer says that occasionally when he is at a stoplight with the transmission in first gear and the clutch pedal depressed, the vehicle will begin to move by itself. Technician A says the problem could be caused by insufficient clutch pedal free play. Technician B says the problem could be caused by an internal leak in the clutch master cylinder. Who is correct?

   a. Technician A
   b. Technician B
   c. Both A and B
   d. Neither A nor B

9. Technician A says transmission noise that is only heard when the vehicle is driven in first gear is probably caused by a bad input shaft bearing. Technician B says noise in first gear only could be caused by bad output shaft bearings. Who is correct?

   a. Technician A
   b. Technician B
   c. Both A and B
   d. Neither A nor B

10. Which of the following would not cause hard shifting?

    a. Worn shift forks
    b. Improperly adjusted clutch
    c. Weak pressure plate
    d. Worn synchronizers

11. Technician A says the transmission may jump out of gear if the transmission is not mounted squarely and securely to the engine. Technician B says excessive input shaft endplay may cause a transmission to jump out of gear. Who is correct?

    a. Technician A
    b. Technician B
    c. Both A and B
    d. Neither A nor B

12. A RWD vehicle exhibits a vibration that is most evident at 32–34 mph. Technician A says that this may be caused by incorrect vehicle height. Technician B says that an improper drive pinion angle may be the cause of this problem. Who is correct?

    a. Technician A
    b. Technician B
    c. Both A and B
    d. Neither A nor B

13. Technician A says the driveline balance should be inspected by a specialty shop. Technician B says if the driveline angles are wrong, the rear axle has moved. Who is correct?

    a. Technician A
    b. Technician B
    c. Both A and B
    d. Neither A nor B

14. While diagnosing a vibration that becomes more noticeable with vehicle speed, Technician A says the driveshaft may be out of balance. Technician B says the tires may be out of balance. Who is correct?

    a. Technician A
    b. Technician B
    c. Both A and B
    d. Neither A nor B

15. Which of the following would be the most likely cause for a heavy vibration that occurs only during hard acceleration?

    a. Worn or sagging rear springs
    b. Incorrect driveshaft balance
    c. Worn U-joints
    d. Worn centering ball and socket in the double Cardan joint

16. A "whirring" noise is coming from the drive axle only when the vehicle is driven straight. Technician A says the differential side gears could be worn. Technician B says the noise could be caused by worn drive pinion gear bearings. Who is correct?

    a. Technician A
    b. Technician B
    c. Both A and B
    d. Neither A nor B

17. The interpretation of a ring and pinion gear contact pattern test is being discussed. Technician A says that excessive toe contact will require that the drive pinion be moved closer to the ring gear. Technician B says that the ideal contact pattern will be centered on the coast side of the ring gear. Who is correct?

    a. Technician A
    b. Technician B
    c. Both A and B
    d. Neither A nor B

18. Which of the following is not a likely cause of a fluid leak at the axle shaft seals in a RWD axle housing?

    a. Incorrect installation of the seal
    b. Damaged companion flange journal
    c. Damaged axle tube
    d. Damaged axle shaft journal

19. Technician A says that clutch drag is caused by a warped disc. Technician B says clutch drag is caused by liquid contaminate on the friction surfaces. Who is correct?

    a. Technician A
    b. Technician B
    c. Both A and B
    d. Neither A nor B

20. Which of the following would not typically cause a rear axle shaft to break?

    a. Incorrect wheel bearing adjustments
    b. Misaligned axle housing
    c. Overloaded vehicle
    d. Slipping clutch